*For Nick, of course* — M. J.    •    *For Kes and Maggie* — V. W.

Text copyright © 2011 by Martin Jenkins • Illustrations copyright © 2011 by Vicky White • All rights reserved. No part of this book may be reproduced, transmitted, or stored in a information retrieval system in any form or by any means, graphic, electronic, or mechanical, including photocopying, taping, and recording, without prior written permission from the publisher. • First U.S. edition 2011 • Library of Congress Cataloging-in-Publication Data

Jenkins, Martin, date.
Can we save the tiger? / Martin Jenkins ; illustrated by Vicky White. — 1st ed.
p.   cm.
ISBN 978-0-7636-4909-8
1. Wildlife conservation — Juvenile literature. 2. Extinction (Biology) — Juvenile literature.
3. Tigers — Conservation — Juvenile literature. I. White, Vicky, ill. II. Title.
QL83. J473 2011
591.68 — dc22          2010008899

Printed in Shenzhen, Guangdong, China • This book was typeset in Bembo. • The illustrations were done in pencil and oil paint. • Candlewick Press, 99 Dover Street, Somerville, Massachusetts 02144 • visit us at www.candlewick.com
11 12 13 14 15 16 CCP 10 9 8 7 6 5 4 3 2

# Can We Save the Tiger?

Martin Jenkins  *illustrated by* Vicky White

CANDLEWICK PRESS

# The world's quite a big place, you know. But it's not *that* big, when you consider how much there is to squeeze into it.

After all, it's home not just to billions of people, but to the most amazing number of other kinds of living things, too. And we're all jostling for space.

We humans have changed the world a lot over the years, to make room for ourselves and to produce the things we need. We've turned forests into farmland, dammed rivers, and built towns and cities to live in.

Some of the other animals and plants that we share the Earth with have coped with the changes very well. But some haven't.

In fact, some have coped so badly that they're not here anymore.

They're extinct.

DODO *Raphus cucullatus*
Where found: *Mauritius, in the Indian Ocean*
Last seen: *Around 1665*

6

That means we'll never see **a live dodo** . . .

STELLER'S
SEA COW
*Hydrodamalis gigas*

Where found:
*North Pacific Ocean*

Last seen: *1768*

or a Steller's
sea cow, or a
marsupial wolf,
or a great auk,
or a broad-faced
potoroo . . .

**MARSUPIAL WOLF**
*Thylacinus cynocephalus*

Where found: *Tasmania*

Last seen: *1936*

**BROAD-FACED POTOROO**
*Potorous platyops*

Where found: *Australia*

Last seen: *1875*

**GREAT AUK**
*Pinguinus impennis*

Where found: *North Atlantic Ocean*

Last seen: *1852*

9

or . . . I could go on and on.

And then there are all those other species that are still around, but only barely.

They're in danger of becoming extinct, just like the dodo and Steller's sea cow.

There are so many endangered species all over the world that it's hard to pick out some special ones.

Still, I'm sure you'll all agree that tigers are pretty special.

**TIGER** *Panthera tigris*

Where found: *Bangladesh, Bhutan, Cambodia, China, India, Indonesia, Laos, Malaysia, Myanmar, Nepal, the Russian Federation, Thailand, and Vietnam*

Size: *Weighs up to 570 pounds and measures up to 12 feet long (the biggest cat in the world)*

Life span: *Up to 20 years in zoos; usually up to 15 or so in the wild*

Habits: *Usually lives in forests and sometimes in grassland, swampy areas, or farmland. Lives alone (except for mothers looking after their young).*

Breeding: *Normally two to four cubs are born. Only the mother looks after them. They stay with her until they are about two years old.*

Eats: *Other animals. Usually hunts at night*

Number left: *Fewer than 2,500 breeding adults in the wild*

Tigers are big and they're beautiful and they're fierce. And all this makes life difficult for them these days.

Because **they're big,** they need a lot of space. But the countries where they live, like India and Indonesia, have huge numbers of people in them too, all trying to make a living and all needing to be fed.

And because **they're beautiful,** people have always hunted them for their skins. They also kill them for their bones and meat to use as medicines.

And because **tigers are fierce,** they don't mix very well with humans. They usually eat deer and antelope and other wild animals, but when there are people nearby, they may end up eating farm animals like cows, sheep, and goats instead. Sometimes (though hardly ever), some tigers, usually old or sick ones, end up eating people too.

So if you were a poor farmer trying to make a living with a couple of cows and a few goats, you might not be too happy if you found there was a hungry tiger living nearby. And if you knew that someone might pay you more for a tiger skin and some bones than you could earn in three whole months working in the fields, then you might find it very tempting to set a trap or two, even if you knew it was against the law.

Perhaps it's not too surprising that there aren't that many tigers left.

ASIAN
ELEPHANT
*Elephas maximus*

Where found:
*South and
Southeast Asia*

SLOTH BEAR *Melursus ursinus*

Where found: *South Asia*

AFRICAN
HUNTING DOG
*Lycaon pictus*
Where found: *Africa*

Many other animals are also running
out of room, including these ones.

But not all endangered species need lots of space.

# Take partula snails. They're tiny—

so small that one of them could happily spend its whole

life in a medium-size bush. And they're not at all scary.

But, like tigers, they're in big trouble, although nobody

really meant to give them a hard time.

**PARTULA SNAILS** *Partula (over 120 species)*

Where found: *Islands in the Pacific Ocean, especially in French Polynesia, where there were originally 63 species. Now only 5 of these are left in the wild, while 11 others survive in zoos. The rest are extinct.*

Size: *Less than 1 inch long*

Life span: *Up to 5 years*

Habits: *Lives in trees and bushes*

Breeding: *Each snail produces one live baby every six to eight weeks.*

Eats: *Plants*

Partula snails live on islands in the Pacific Ocean, miles from anywhere. There are lots of different kinds, and they've been here for millions of years.

When the first people arrived on the islands hundreds of years ago, the partula snails didn't seem to mind too much and just got on with their lives, feeding on leaves in the forests.

Then, about a hundred years ago, people brought a different kind of snail to the islands. This was the giant African land snail.

They brought it because it's good to eat—it makes especially delicious snail soup—and is very easy to look after.

The giant African land snails took well to the islands, and soon there were tons of them, many more than anyone wanted to eat. And it turned out that they had pretty healthy appetites themselves. Soon they were chomping their way through people's crops as if there was no tomorrow.

Something had to be done.

## GIANT AFRICAN LAND SNAIL *Achatina fulica*

Where found: *Originally East Africa, now many different parts of the world, including Asia, South America, the West Indies, and islands in the Pacific Ocean*

Unfortunately what people decided to do was to introduce a *third* kind of snail. This one was called the **rosy euglandina,** and its favorite food was . . . other snails.

The idea was that the rosy euglandina would feed on the giant African land snails and stop them from eating everyone's crops.

This worked a bit, but not that well — there are still plenty of the giant snails on the islands. The problem was that the rosy euglandinas thought that the partula snails — which weren't doing anyone any harm — were the most delicious snack and quickly started eating them all up instead.

Now there are hardly any partula snails at all. Some kinds have become extinct, some now live only in zoos, and a few still hang on in places that the rosy euglandina hasn't managed to reach yet.

ROSY EUGLANDINA
*Euglandina rosea*

Where found: *Originally Florida, now introduced to French Polynesia, New Guinea, Hawaii, the Philippines, and other islands in the Pacific Ocean*

**QUOKKA** *Setonix brachyurus*

Where found: *Australia*

Attacked by: *Foxes and cats*

**MARIANA FRUIT DOVE** *Ptilinopus roseicapilla*

Where found: *Mariana Islands, Pacific Ocean (now extinct on Guam)*

Attacked by: *Brown tree snake*

**GROUND IGUANAS** *Cyclura (nine species)*
Where found: *West Indies*
Attacked by: *Cats, dogs, pigs, rats, and mongooses*

Other animals, including these ones, are also affected by predators that have been introduced by people.

Ugly things can be endangered, too.

Perhaps I'm being unfair, but I don't think many people would call vultures exactly beautiful.

But they are definitely very useful animals. They eat carrion — the bodies of animals that have already died — which means they do a very good job of keeping places clean.

## WHITE-RUMPED VULTURE
*Gyps bengalensis*

Where found: *Bangladesh, Bhutan, Cambodia, India, Laos, Myanmar, Nepal, Pakistan, Thailand, and Vietnam*

Size: *Weighs up to 16 pounds; wings measure 6 feet across*

Life span: *Up to 20 years*

Habits: *Mostly lives on farmland and in cities and villages. Nests in big groups in trees or on clifftops or buildings.*

Breeding: *Each female lays one egg a year. The chick is fed by both its parents and stays in the nest until it is three months old.*

Eats: *Carrion*

Number left: *Fewer than 10,000*

In India, until recently, there were millions of vultures, and they mostly fed on the bodies of cows that had died in the countryside. A while ago, people began to notice that there were a lot fewer vultures around than they remembered. But they weren't being hunted, and there were still places for them to nest and plenty of dead cows for them to eat. People also noticed that the vultures they *did* see, perched on trees or buildings, often looked all droopy and miserable, as if they were sick. Was there some disease, like vulture-measles or flu, spreading across India?

It wasn't that, but it took some detective work to find out what the problem was: farmers were giving their cows a kind of medicine that was very poisonous to vultures. When the vultures fed on the body of a cow that had been given the medicine, they got sick and died.

Now that everyone knows what the problem is, maybe something can be done about it. People can try to persuade the government to stop that particular medicine from being sold and can try to explain to farmers why it shouldn't be used.

But it's never as simple as that. The companies that make the medicine will lose out on the money they get from selling it and may try to persuade the government not to do anything—who cares about a few ugly vultures, anyway? And even if it's not being made anymore, there will still be lots of it around, in stores all over the country and in farmers' cupboards. Getting everyone everywhere to stop using it is really difficult. And by the time that's happened, it may be too late for the wild vultures.

These animals have also become accidentally endangered by human actions or disease.

### SAWFISHES

*Family* Pristidae *(seven species)*

Where found: *Near the coast in warm parts of the Atlantic, Indian, and Pacific Oceans*

Problem: *Accidentally caught in fishing nets set for other types of fish*

## ALBATROSSES
*Family* Diomedeidae
*(21 species)*

Where found: *Cold parts of the ocean in the Southern Hemisphere*

Problem: *Accidentally caught on fishing hooks set to catch tuna and other big fish*

## EUROPEAN CRAYFISH *Astacus astacus*

Where found: *Rivers and streams in Europe*

Problem: *Affected by crayfish plague caught from introduced North American crayfish*

## GOLDEN ARROW POISON FROG
*Atelopus zeteki*

Where found: *Panama*

Problem: *Affected by a skin disease that people have probably helped spread*

Sometimes, though, we have managed to do the right thing in time.

There are quite a lot of species that have nearly gone extinct and that we have saved, at least for the time being.

One of these is the American bison.

## AMERICAN BISON *Bison bison*

Where found: *Canada and the United States*

Size: *Weighs up to 2,000 pounds; measures up to 6½ feet tall at the shoulder and 10 feet in length. Males are bigger than females.*

Life span: *Up to 40 years in zoos; usually 15–20 years in the wild*

Habits: *Lives on prairies and in woods. Forms huge herds on prairies but usually lives in small groups in woods.*

Breeding: *Females have one calf a year. The calf stays with its mother until it is about one year old.*

Eats: *Grass and other low-growing plants*

Number left: *More than 500,000*

The American bison is the biggest land animal in North America. A few hundred years ago, there were millions of them roaming the prairies and woodlands. Native people hunted them for their meat and skins, but they didn't kill too many, so there were always plenty around.

Then Europeans arrived with their horses and guns, and things began to change. They killed huge numbers of bison for their skins, they plowed up parts of the prairies to plant wheat, and they turned the rest into ranches where they could graze cattle. All this left less and less room for the bison. Suddenly there were just two small herds of wild bison left, and a few kept in pens by ranchers. The bison was in danger of becoming extinct, without anyone really noticing.

# Luckily, people did begin to take notice, and at the last minute they started to do things.

The ranchers who kept the captive bison started breeding from them, and governments set up reserves to protect the wild herds. Bison numbers began to grow; now there are hundreds of thousands again. Most of them are still kept by ranchers, who treat them like cattle, but there are also some wild herds. There are still nowhere near as many as there once were, but there are enough for us not to have to worry about them going extinct anytime soon.

These animals were all once endangered
but are now doing well.

WHITE RHINOCEROS
*Ceratotherium simum*

Where found: *Eastern
and southern Africa*

Number left: *Only around 20
survived at the
end of the
nineteenth
century.
Now around
17,500.*

**VICUÑA** *Vicugna vicugna*

Where found: *The Andes Mountains in South America*

Number left: *Reduced to a few thousand in the 1960s. Now around 350,000.*

**ANTARCTIC FUR SEAL**
*Arctocephalus gazella*

Where found: *Cold parts of the ocean in the Southern Hemisphere*

Number left: *Nearly extinct at the end of the nineteenth century; now four to six million. Almost all of them breed on South Georgia in the Atlantic Ocean.*

Bison are actually quite easy animals to look after. As long as you don't hunt them and make sure they've got a reasonable amount of space, they pretty much take care of themselves.

Not all endangered species are like that, though. Some you can't take your eye off for a minute. The kakapo is one of these.

Kakapos are amazing birds that live in New Zealand. They are huge dumpy parrots that can't fly and come out only at night.

They live as long as people do, they're fussy about what they eat (like a lot of people), and they usually only breed once every three or four years, when their favorite trees produce a bumper crop of fruit and seeds.

**KAKAPO** *Strigops habroptila*

Where found: *New Zealand*

Size: *Weighs up to 9 pounds; measures up to 24 inches long*

Life span: *Probably more than 60 years*

Habits: *Lives in woodland and grassland. Feeds at night. Doesn't fly, but sort of jogs along.*

Breeding: *Female lays up to three eggs at a time. Only the mother looks after the chicks when they hatch. Chicks stay in the nest until they are 10–12 weeks old.*

Eats: *Fruit, seeds, flowers, plant shoots, and sap from trees*

Number left: *124 (at the last count)*

The trouble is that because kakapos can't fly, they are easy prey for animals like rats, dogs, cats, and stoats that like to eat them or their eggs. Before people arrived on New Zealand, there were none of these predators there and lots of kakapos. Then, about 1,500 years ago, people started coming, bringing these animals with them, some by accident (like rats) and some on purpose (like dogs and, later, cats and stoats). The kakapos got rarer and rarer. At one point, people thought they might be extinct. Then a handful were discovered in the far south, but there were cats and stoats there, too, and every year there were fewer kakapos.

Conservationists decided to catch as many of the survivors as possible and put them on small islands, out of reach of predators. That worked, but unfortunately the kakapos hardly ever bred. More were dying, of old age and in accidents, than were hatching out.

# By 1995, there were just 51 alive in the world.

Since then people have redoubled their efforts to try to save the kakapo. They guard the islands to make sure no predators arrive. They've put collars with radio transmitters on the kakapos to keep track of them. They've given them extra food to try to persuade them to breed, and when they do breed, they keep an eye on the nests using remote-controlled cameras. They've even put heaters over the nests to make sure the eggs or chicks don't get too cold when their mother is off feeding at night. It's all working, and very, very slowly, the number of kakapos is growing. By 2010, there were over 120 kakapos—still hardly any, but more than 51.

These are some of the animals that have been brought back from the brink of extinction but are still very rare.

## RODRIGUES FLYING FOX
*Pteropus rodricensis*

Where found: *Rodrigues Island, in the Indian Ocean*

Number left: *In 1979, only about 70 survived. The population reached 5,000 in 2002 but went down to 4,000 or so in 2003, when a cyclone hit Rodrigues.*

## WHOOPING CRANE
*Grus americana*

Where found: *North America*

Number left: *In 1938, only 15 adult birds survived. By the end of 2007, there were 382 birds in the wild and 148 in zoos.*

## BERMUDA PETREL
*Pterodroma cahow*

Where found: *Bermuda*

Number left: *Thought extinct for 300 years but rediscovered in the 1950s breeding on small islands. Numbers have gone up from 18 pairs in 1951 to around 250 birds now.*

So you see, trying to save just one endangered species like the kakapo can be hard work, and there are thousands of them altogether. What's more, saving species is going to get more complicated. We haven't just changed the world in obvious ways, like cutting down forests and building roads — we're changing the climate, too. And that affects everything everywhere.

Because of climate change, places like the Arctic that haven't been affected very much by people up till now are starting to change fast, and that means that some animals that we thought were safe — like polar bears — are now in trouble.

When it comes to looking after all the species that are already endangered, there's such a lot to do that sometimes it might all seem to be too much, especially when there are so many other important things to worry about. But if we stop trying, the chances are that pretty soon we'll end up with a world where there are no tigers or elephants, or sawfishes or whooping cranes, or albatrosses or ground iguanas.

## And I think that would be a shame, don't you?

**POLAR BEAR**
*Ursus maritimus*

Where found: *Arctic regions of Canada, Greenland, Norway, the Russian Federation, and the United States*

Number left: *20,000–25,000*

# Find out more online

Scientists and conservationists have made a list of about 17,000 animals and plants that they think are in danger. The list includes one in five of all the world's mammals and nearly one in three of all amphibians.

You can find the list, along with information about where the species live and why they are endangered, on the website **www.iucnredlist.org.**

The website **www.arkive.org** also has information on a lot of endangered species, including pictures and some great video clips.

Organizations around the world are working to protect endangered species. They all have websites that tell you what they're up to. Here are some of them:

*BirdLife International*: **www.birdlife.org**

*Conservation International*: **www.conservation.org**

*Durrell Wildlife Conservation Trust*: **www.durrell.org**

*Fauna and Flora International*: **www.fauna-flora.org**

*International Union for Conservation of Nature (IUCN)*: **www.iucn.org**

*The Nature Conservancy*: **www.nature.org**

*Wildlife Conservation Society*: **www.wcs.org**

*World Wildlife Fund*: **www.wwf.org**

# Index

SANDER'S SLIPPER ORCHID
*Paphiopedilum sanderianum*

Where found: *Sarawak, northwestern Borneo*

*Discovered in 1885; thought extinct until rediscovered in 1978. Still very rare, but protected in a national park.*